Self Love

I0407625

The 10 Pillars of Self Love

Katy Richards

2

Table of Contents

Introduction

Self love is a concept that a lot of us may have some troubles with. We are often used to showing love to other people we are close to and making sure that they feel good all the time, but it is hard to give that same kind of love right back to ourselves sometimes. Over time, when we choose to ignore ourselves and not give the love and attention that we deserve back to ourselves, it is going to make other parts of our lives and relationships and can make it hard to do the things that we want.

Learning how to love ourselves can be hard. We feel that we don't deserve this love, that we aren't good enough to have this love, that we need to try and work harder before anyone can even like us, much less love us. We may have some of these negative thoughts going through our minds on a regular basis, we may not spend any time on ourselves, and we may not even be able to slow down and say no on occasion because we figure that others are more important to us. This can wear you down in no time and make all the stress and negative thoughts take over your life.

Here, we are going to take a look at some of the steps that you can take, the ten pillars, in order to have more self love. It is impossible to provide attention and love to others in the proper way if we can't even love ourselves. When you learn how to open yourself up to love, you can feel better, have more energy, and be better capable of managing your time and getting everything that you want out of life. Let's learn how to love ourselves so that we can be the best version of ourselves possible.

Chapter 1: Embrace Your Uniqueness

Every person is unique. We all have special traits that make us different from others, different ways of talking, different ways of acting, different strengths, and even differences in our physical appearances. This is all a part of who we are and it makes us special. This should be something that we celebrate, but in our current world, most of us have insecurities because we don't fit in with what the media and others tell us is normal.

This can lead to a lot of issues with your levels of confidence. When you spend all of your time worried about what other people think about you, and worry that you don't fit in, it is hard to feel good about yourself. You can see the issues in all of the magazines that come out, the television shows, and even on the news. We look anywhere and we see the issue with the super thin models, the stories that tell us how we need to dress and how we should behave. We see the glamorous lifestyles of all those celebrities and even the people in your favorite shows, and we feel bad when we are not able to reach this high point.

But why do we want to be like these other people so much? The stories that we see in the magazines and on the television are all made up, there to just entertain us and not really the reality that we should be living. And even if some people do look better on television than us or may be better at some things that us, we have our own unique traits that shouldn't be ignored.

When we start to realize how important and valuable we are, it is easier to be happy. We may not be as good as someone else in some things, but there are still many great features and traits that we can bring to the table. We may not make a ton of money, but we provide for our family and love them. We may not be drop dead gorgeous, but we are a good friend and a good listener to others around us. Just because we may not be as good at something as we wish, that doesn't mean that we aren't amazing at other things and it is these other things that we should be focusing on.

How did we get off course?

The big question here is to understand why we feel that our uniqueness is not that important to us anymore. Why do we focus so much of our energy being upset that we are not like someone else? The root of this problem is that subconsciously, we are looking to figure out the true meaning of life, and often we are going to use this as our way to find happiness. Society is good at teaching us that when we follow the norms that would make us like others, we are going to be happy. But being just like everyone else is not going to make us happy and in fact, it can make us feel miserable because we are sure to fail.

- There are a number of problems that come from being the same as everyone else in society. We are stuck with seeking other people for approval and in the outside world to feel good, rather than looking to ourselves. But when everyone else is concerned with themselves, they will find that the world is ready to disappoint. Some of the issues with looking outward for our own meaning includes:

- We are always seeking the approval of others so that we can feel valued.

- We are always in a competition with others in order to get into the best schools, the best job, and more.

- We are going to look for a partner that we expect to complete us and give us some self-worth, rather than focusing on finding someone who is good for us.

- We will strive to make more money so that we are able to buy some things that will make us happy.

- We will work hard in order to stay youthful and looking young, valuing our youth more than we do wisdom and age.

When we are going for just these kinds of goals, you will find that your happiness is not going to be there. It is elusive because we are focusing on the wrong things in life, forgetting to enjoy ourselves and to keep the important things at the forefront. We may feel that we found that happiness, but it doesn't take long to realize that this was a temporary condition. Soon is it going to slip again and we will have to keep on searching to find that happiness again.

How to get out of this

Changing our direction is going to take some work, but your life is important. You may find that making these changes can be uncomfortable at first, but soon you will be able to find the true happiness that you want and you will feel better. First, you need to look at the bullets above and determine if you are following someone else's path or your own. If you are on a different path, you are in trouble because you will never find the happiness that you need. Get out of that mold and celebrate who you are as a person.

If you are trying to get your self-worth and approval from others, it is time to stop doing this and find these qualities inside of yourself. If you aren't happy with the career that you are in, it is time to make some changes (even if this means getting some new skills) so that you are able to follow your passion, rather than just make an income.

There is something unique in each of us, we just need to learn how to embrace this. It doesn't matter if we are the same as other people or if we are missing out on something that we have convinced ourselves is important. There is something that is unique in all of us, and we just need to find what it is and then let it shine each day!

Chapter 2: Learn Your Strengths

Sometimes the issues that come up with our self love is because we don't know our own strengths and weaknesses. Many of us don't want to admit that we have issues that we need to deal with or that we are dealing with weaknesses because we feel this makes us lacking or bad in some manner. But when we try to force something to happen that isn't there, we are going to end up in trouble. Often we won't admit that we aren't able to do something, and then we feel bad and like a failure when we aren't able to do that activity.

It is a good idea to learn what our weaknesses are so that we can focus more on our strengths and what will get us ahead. Just because we are not that great at some things doesn't make us less of a person, we just need to understand that everyone has things that they may lack in and some things that they are good at. If you focus on the things that you are bad at, you are going to be continuously disappointed in what is going on in your life. On the other hand, if you focus on the good things that you can do, you will feel good all of the time.

Understanding the weaknesses

If you are like most people, you will probably spend a huge amount of your time focusing on your weaknesses. You will know what you can't do and be worried that this makes you inadequate or makes it so that others are judging you in bad ways. But when you spend all this time focusing on your weaknesses, which are often things that you are not able to control, you are going to run into a lot of issues with your self-esteem and you may have trouble even getting started with self love.

In reality, everyone has some weaknesses that they are dealing with. The difference between you and some of these other people though is that some of them know how to avoid their weaknesses and just focus on the good things that they are able to do. They won't run out and try to do the things they are bad at because they know that this is going to go badly for them and they refuse to let these weaknesses take over their lives.

When you focus on the weaknesses and all the things that you are not able to do, you are inviting depression, low self-esteem, and other issues to your life. Yes, there are things that you are not able to do, but you need to just let those go and focus on doing things that are good for you, focusing on your strengths, and you will see such a big difference.

But we are going to take just a moment to focus on these weaknesses, in order to help you out. For this one, write down some of the weaknesses that you have, ones that you are not able to do anything about because they just can't be improved. But the next step is important. In addition to writing down the weaknesses, write down a positive thing that you are able to do to counteract that weakness.

When that is done, write down some tips on what you are able to do to avoid these weaknesses. If they are things that you are running into on a daily basis, it is going to cause some issues on your psyche. It may be time to consider taking on a different role at work, asking for a new project that can go to your strengths, or making some other changes so that you are able to get away from that negativity of focusing on your weaknesses and instead find something that will let you focus on your strengths.

Understanding your strengths

It doesn't matter who you are, you have some special strengths that you can work with. You may not have a lot of money, but you may be generous and know how to make some great gifts on a budget. You may have trouble with talking to people, but you will be able to write out some beautiful words and can tell stories in written form compared to other people. You may not be able to run a business, but you are able to come up with innovative ideas to help keep your company doing well.

There are many different strengths and just because you are not able to do some things doesn't mean that you aren't valuable. And you may even have some of the strengths that other people are jealous of and wish they had. We spend to much time concentrating on the things that we can't do, we often forget about the good things that we are able to do, and we let this cloud our judgment.

To start out with this one, take a few minutes and write down all of the things that you are good at. Don't sit there and think "yeah, I'm good at this thing, but someone else can do it better." You need to just focus on the things that you think you bring to the table. You will be surprised at how hard this can be, but aim to put down a list of at least five to ten things.

Now keep this paper somewhere that you are able to keep track of and look at on a regular basis. When you start to feel a bit low about yourself or that you are just not as good at things as someone else, it is time to bring out this paper and look it over. It is a good way to remind yourself that you do bring something to the table and that you are just as valuable as anyone else.

When you truly learn what your strengths are and how to avoid the weaknesses that you have, it is much easier to love all the good about yourself. It is never a good idea to focus too much on the stuff that you can't do, or can't do well, because there may be nothing that you can do about this. But when you learn how to love yourself and love all of the great things that you can do, you will find that some of that low self-esteem and other issues will go away.

Chapter 3: Ignore Those Inner Demons

Those inner demons that are inside of you will make things hard. They are the ones that are telling you that you aren't worth the effort of other people liking you. They are the ones that are telling you that you aren't good looking enough, that you aren't thin enough, or that you don't have enough money or something else. These inner demons are big liars, but they will make you miserable all of the time.

First, we need to take some time to figure out what our inner demons may be. We need to understand what lies we are telling ourselves and teach ourselves that these lies are just not true. If we feel that we are not pretty enough, it may be because the media and television shows are telling us that we need to look a certain way and the mirror is telling us that we don't look this way. If we are not thin enough, we may be seeing others who are fitter and look better, and feel guilty abut the way that we look. If we are not successful enough, we may see other people getting promotions at work and other places, and then feel that we are being left behind because we are not getting the attention that we think that we deserve for our hard work.

The biggest issue with working on our inner demons is that even though we may feel that they are false at times, we can find all of these proofs that will tell us that these demons are right. As you can see from the examples above, there is always something that can be our proof. And this can make it harder for you to fight them off and realize that your life is happier without those demons in your life.

So the first step that you need to figure out is what the inner demon is for you. You may think that you are pretty, but you are worried about being too poor or not as fit as you should. Each person is going to have a lot of different demons and you need to learn which ones are bothering you so that you can make them go away.

Once you figure out what demon is bothering you, or demons, you will be able to fight them off a little bit better. Each time that you hear the demon telling you something like you don't matter or you are not pretty enough, try to challenge it a little bit. Stop that thought in its track and tell it that you no longer believe it. You may find that you are challenging yourself quite a bit when you first get started, but over time, your mind will quit letting these demons in and it is easier to fight them off and feel better.

If you find that just telling these demons that they are wrong is too hard for you, it is time to change it up. Starting some positive thinking is one of the best options that you need to make this easier. For example, any time that you start to think that you're not pretty, you will stop that thought and think of something that you are good at, such as a good friend or a good listener. Over time you will be able to turn around some of these negative thoughts and make them a little more positive, and this can do some wonders for your self worth and eventually it can help you to increase your self love as well.

Chapter 4: Find People Who Lift You Up

One of the things that you should realize when it comes to working on self love is that you need to hang around the right kind of people. The type of people you hang out with will greatly determine your mood and how much you love yourself. Most of us may not realize it, but if we are dealing with low self-esteem and issues with loving ourselves, it may be due to the fact that we are hanging out with the wrong kind of people.

There are two kind of people that you can choose to spend your time with. The first group is the complainers and the gossipers. These are the people who rarely ever get out there and do anything, but they sure do spend a lot of time complaining about all the stuff that is going wrong in their lives. They are never happy and never bring each other up; rather, when something goes well for someone in this group, the others will just wallow in pity that they aren't doing as well either. The second group is a much livelier group. These people boost each other up, are there for each other whether you are up or down, and find things other than gossip to talk about when you are all together.

There are several different things that are going to happen based on the type of group that you hang out with. In the first group, you are going to find that your self-esteem is very low. You will spend all your time feeling down because this group rarely talks about anything positive. This is a very negative group, talking down about other people and always complaining about their lives. They don't bring up anything positive because they don't feel like there is anything positive in their lives. Any time that you do something that is unique or special, this group is not going to applaud you; often they will try to bring you down and mock your success because they don't like the idea that you are doing something they aren't. This can be a really negative and toxic group to hang out with and if you are looking to increase your self-love, it is time to find a new group.

On the other hand, the second group can do so much for your self-esteem. They realize that bringing each other down all of the time is not a good way to live. When you are trying to reach a goal, they are going to be right there, ready to cheer you on and get you to work even harder than before. When you are successful, they are going to be right there to applaud and make you feel good. They may be a bit tough because they don't allow you to fail, unlike the first group, but they know all of the good and strength that is inside of you, and they aren't going to let you settle for less.

Out of these two groups, the second group is going to be the one that you should be spending your time on. This is the group that is there for you and will help you to feel so much better than before. If you are serious about adding some self love to your life, you need to take a close look at the group of friends that you are around and see whether they are there to bring you up or if they are tearing you down. If you are actually looking to increase your self love, it is likely that your group of friends is in the first group.

If your friends are in that first group, it is time to make a change. You need to learn how to love yourself enough to realize that you are worth so much more than that first group of friends. You deserve to go for those goals that you want. You deserve to have a good and happy life and to reach your goals and dreams without someone trying to bring you down. And once you start to make some changes to the group of people that you hang out with on a regular basis so that you have some of the love and support you need during this time.

Where can I find people to lift me up?

At this point, you may understand some of the importance of finding some new friends and new people to hang out with, but you may be worried that you aren't going to be able to make the switch from the group that you hang out with to some that are new to you. Luckily, if you are willing to step out of your comfort zone just a little bit, you will find that there are actually quite a few places you can search in order to find some new positive friends.

The first thing that you should do is look into some of your hobbies and see if here are any groups there that you can meet with. If you like to read, join a book club If you like to sew, join a sewing club. You can do this with any of the hobbies that you like to spend time with. Not only do you get to spend some time doing something that you love, but you are likely to meet others who like the same things that you do and this can be a great starting point for a new friendship.

Going to events in your community is another great way to make some new friends. If you have a town hall meeting, this is a good place to start or something similar. You will be able to learn a bit more about some of the issues that are facing your town and community at the time and you can also meet some new people at the same time.

Checking out some of the groups at your school (or the school that your kids attend if that is where you are) or at your church can be great. You will have something in common there and will have a regular place that you can meet up in case things get too busy to do this elsewhere. It might even give you an excuse to get more involved in what is going on in the school or the church, and just that involvement, along with some of the great people that you will meet and the interaction that you get with others will make a big difference in the amount of self love that you will give to yourself.

There are so many places where you will be able to meet some of these positive and upbeat people that you need to help you to get rid of the old crowd and some of the negative thoughts that are going on in your head, and bring in some new people who will be your supporters and are much more fun to hang out with. take a look around your community and see if there are any new groups, or at least any that interest you, and take a chance at meeting them. You would be surprised at how easy it is to meet some new people and to feel good about yourself if you just take a chance and put yourself out there.

Chapter 5: Do Things That You Love

Take a moment and think about your day. What was one of the first things that you did when you woke up? Think from the earliest point of the day and go through everything that you did until this point, or go on and think of all the things that you will do until you get to bed that night. Once you are done with today, go back over each of the days for the past week and think of all the activities that you did.

Now, when you are done, you will probably realize that you were really busy during that time. Some of the motions may have been pretty routine by this point, things that you do the same all of the time. Some of the things were for your children or for your spouse, helping to get things done for them so that their day went more smoothly. Some of the things that you did were for your boss or for your job so that you could have money and take care of the necessities. You may have run errands, helped with homework, done the dishes and cleaned up the house, went to activities and appointments, and so much more. But if you take a closer look, there may notice that there is something really important that is missing from your day.

On any of the days that you went and thought through, did you spend any time on yourself? Outside of a quick shower and getting dressed, did you spend any time doing something for yourself? Did you spend some time reading a book that you like, doing a workout to help yourself feel better, doing some art, taking a warm bath?

Too many times we don't spend some time helping ourselves to feel better. We are too worried abut taking care of everyone else, making sure that they are all set up to go about our day, but if we get two seconds to take a deep breath before we head to bed, it is almost like we feel guilty about this attention. But how are you supposed to feel good about yourself, how are you supposed to keep away the depression and the other issues, if you don't spend at least a little bit of time on ourselves each day.

You are never too busy to fit in something that is good for your body and your mind, no matter what you are telling yourself. Even ten minutes of doing an activity that you enjoy is going to make a big change in your outlook on life and it will make it easier to love yourself when you are relaxed when you can let go of the stress, compared to continuing on this mad run all over the place.

The activity that you do is not really that important. You get to decide what activity sounds like the most fun for you, what one is going to make you feel happy and satisfied. If you need a few minutes to relax after chasing the kids and a stressful day at work, draw a warm bath and add in some scented candles and Epsom salts to help you to feel good. If you need to reduce your stress levels overall, you may find that going for a walk with your family after supper can help to clear out the mind and will make you feel really good. If you love to escape reality each day and read some fantasy, you can save a few minutes each day to help you to read a book that you enjoy. Some people like to do some writing, some like to play some games, and some like to bake. The activity is not as important because you need to pick the thing that is going to be the most relaxing and most valuable to you.

Your goal for the next week is to pick out the activity that sounds the most relaxing to you, and then make time for it each day. This activity can be anything that you would like and you can even pick a different one for the different days of the week if this is better for you (or if you would like to experiment a little bit) to find the right ones. The important thing here is that you spend about twenty minutes or so on the activity each day. It doesn't matter how you have to get to it, doesn't matter how busy you get, put it on your schedule and make sure that you do it each day.

In just a week, you are going to notice such a difference when it comes to how great you feel. It doesn't have to be a lot of time on a daily basis, but it is hard to love yourself if you don't spend any time on yourself. Adding in this small thing into your daily routine is going to make you feel important and can help you to start to love yourself again.

Chapter 6: Stop Those Negative Thoughts

Negative thoughts are often going to be your downfall when it comes to loving yourself. These negative thoughts are found in all of us in this modern world. We are led to believe that we are supposed to look and act a certain way, but this is almost impossible. We aren't able to look like the people in the magazines, we can't be the perfect parent, and not all of us can start our own businesses and be one of the richest people in the world. This is just not possible, but that doesn't mean that we aren't great people, that we don't have our own unique personalities and things to bring to the table. The problem is that some of these negative thoughts are going to keep this away from you.

Getting rid of these negative thoughts can be tough though. Most of us have been dealing with these negative thoughts for many years, maybe the majority of our lives, and making them go away can seem impossible. But if you would like a chance to start feeling better and loving yourself again, you need to make sure that those negative thoughts are all gone.

Take a trip through your mind

One trick that you may find useful when you are working on getting rid of those negative thoughts is visualization. For this one, we are going to sit back and pretend that we are inside of a grocery store. Try to picture all of the different items that are on one shelf inside your mind and then also think about the order that you see them in. You don't have to make this all about the groceries either; thinking that you are in a bookstore or looking through music helps as well.

You don't have to spend a lot of time doing this, about thirty seconds or so, but any time that one of those negative thoughts start to come back into your mind, you should do a short little session of this again. You may find in the beginning that you will need to do this quite a bit because there are so many different thoughts that are negative going through your head. But over time, you are going to get better at this and it is going to be easier. Then when negative thoughts come up in the future, it won't be as big of a deal because you can go right back to this method.

Keep company that is positive

This is like the idea that e talked about before, but if you aren't able to get rid of some of these negative thoughts and feelings that you are having, it could have a lot to do with the type of people you are hanging out with. a study done at Notre Dame in 2013 found that it wasn't uncommon for people to pick up the habits that their roommates had, especially when it came to negative thoughts and traits. Often these negative thoughts are easy to mirror because they will involve thinking and worrying about things out loud.

This means that if you are always thinking some of these negative thoughts that are bringing you down, it may be time to change up the company you are hanging around with. if you keep being around the same people who are making you act this way, it is going to become really hard to change around your negative outlook for something more positive.

Replace the negative with a positive

The next time that you notice that you are dealing with some negative thoughts, it is time to take a step back and figure out why you are dealing with this negative thought. Is it something that is true? Do you really believe this thought, or is it something that you have held onto for a long time and you just aren't able to make go away? Once you recognize some of negative thoughts that are there, it is possible to put in some positive ones instead.

These positive thoughts are going to be kind of hard to work with in the beginning. They are going to force you to challenge and recognize those negative thoughts even more than before, and when you are able to do this, you can put in a positive one in their place. Instead of thinking that you are not as pretty as someone else, you can replace that with a thought about how great your hair was managed today or about how you got the lead on a project at work. There are so many positive things that can be said about you, no matter who you are, you just need to learn how to substitute these in for the negative ones in order to make yourself feel better and to learn how to deal with your self love.

Throw them away

It can sometimes sound a bit crazy, but in this activity, we are going to learn how to clear out our heads of these negative thoughts by throwing them away. With this one, when the nagging thoughts are just not giving you the break that you deserve, you will sit down and write them out on a piece of paper. When you are done, crumple up that piece of paper and throw it away in the trash. This may not seem like it is doing much, but research has shown that doing this helps you to feel better and can improve your positive self image for the rest of the day.

Sometimes all that you need is to let some of these negative thoughts out so that they can't just keep bothering you inside your head. And then the physical act of throwing them away, even though you are just dealing with a piece of paper, can be therapeutic to some and helps them to get things back on track again.

Drink some tea

There are many different reasons that you are dealing with negative thoughts on a daily basis, but if you are dealing with these negative thoughts and they make you feel lonely, a good way to get some comfort is by warming up. In 2012, researches from Yale found that people who were holding onto a hot back recalled having fewer feelings that were negative about their lonely experiences in the past. Drinking some hot tea can give you not only that warm feeling that you want, but ensure that you are getting some healthy antioxidants as well.

One thing to keep in mind with this is that the physical warmth is just supposed to be a quick fix. It does work well, but you should never use this as a substitute for real human interaction. Nothing compares to that and trying to get it to work is just going to make you feel miserable. But if you need a little pick me up at the end of the day, this can really help.

Reframe the situation

If you have the urge to wallow in things not going the right way to or always feel bad for yourself, it is time to stop this. But of course it isn't going to be easy – otherwise, you would have already done it. One thing that you can try out is to reframe the situation. Instead of being upset that a situation is going badly, think of all the good stuff that come with it. For example, if you get a flight that is delayed at the airport, instead of focusing on how late you are running and how it means more time in the airport, think about it as a time to call someone you haven't kept up with in a long time or as a time to get a bit of work done before heading on your way.

You are able to change up any of the experiences that you are dealing with; you just need to learn how to get it done. Sometimes this is harder than others, but with a little bit of work, you are able to make any situation into a good one. Try it a few times, no matter how bleak the situation may be, and you are sure to see some differences in no time at all!

Negative thoughts can be your downfall when it comes to how you react to the world around you. It is really hard to love yourself when that inner critic is always telling you that something is wrong with you or that there is a reason that no one wants to be around you all of the time. But when you follow some of the steps that are above and you will be able to start kicking some of those negative thoughts to the curb while making yourself feel so much better!

Chapter 7: Set Up Some Goals for Yourself

How are you supposed to learn how to love yourself if you don't have any goals in place? Goals are what propel you to keep working hard, to try and reach your best self in the long run. Without these goals, we kind of get into a routine, without any real idea of where we should be going. We list around, hoping that we will have something just land in our laps, but we get severely disappointed when this doesn't happen. Without a goal, we are without a purpose, and this is not a good way to learn how to love ourselves.

Setting goals can make all the difference. It helps us to finally have that purpose that we need to feel happy and ready to take on the day. It allows us to feel good about ourselves because we know what we need to do each day. And when we finally reach that goal, there is no better feeling in the whole wide world. Here we are going to look at some of the important information that you need in order to set up some great goals for yourself so that you can keep progressing forward and keep on being the best version of yourself possible.

What is goal setting?

The first thing we need to look at is what is a goal and what isn't a goal. You aren't able to set a goal that is achievable if you don't even know what the goal is in the first place. For example, what is the main difference between a goal and a resolution?

A resolution is a bit different because it is an intention of waiting for a new plan. When we make these resolutions each year, we are pretty much just writing out a big wish list and some of them may be achievable while others are not. Until we decide to take some action and actually do something about them, these are just lists on a page that have nothing attached to them.

But in goal setting, we are actually taking some of those resolutions and coming up with a plan for them. They are no longer wishes that are on a list, but they are full blown ideas that we want to achieve. Basically, goal setting is going to be the process of deciding what you would like to accomplish and then devising a plan so that you are able to achieve the results that you would like. The resolutions that you make each year are pretty passive, but when they turn into actual goals, they become more active.

Notice in here that we also included that a goal was to achieve a desired result. The implication with this is that we want to make some change sin our behaviors and our current circumstances. The goal setting is where we will plan for our future and what we ant to happen, and then we are going to make the changes that we need to get the outcome that we want.

How to set these goals

The first step that you will need to do in order to get started with goal setting is to choose how to set these right goals. You are able to set any kind of goal that you would like, but remember that it needs to be something that you are able to succeed at, even if it may be a bit of a challenge, and there need to be some action steps that come with it. Some of the steps that you will need to do in order to work on the goal include:

- Determine the goal: what would you like to achieve in the next year, five years, or more. Is it something that you are able to do realistically (remember that what one person is able to do is not always the same as what other people may want to do). The goal should be personal to your life, such as having a family, saving for a vacation, or getting a promotion at work.

- Break it up into smaller pieces: it is not a good idea for you to just have the one goal and then work just on that part. This is going to make you get discouraged because it can take a long time to get to that end goal. Rather, we need to break it down into manageable pieces that, when they are all put together, will help you to reach your end goal. Divide each goal into at least three or four parts (you can do more if needed) and set some dates and expectations for each one.

- Keep the information where you can see it: you need to be constantly reminded of these goals so that you don't give up. You should put them by your bed at night, on the fridge, or in the bathroom so you see them as you get ready in the morning. You can write out something that will remind you and motivate you towards the goals, or write out the steps that you are doing to reach the goal as a constant reminder.

- Make adjustments: there are going to be times when your goals are not going quite as planned, and it is fine to make some adjustments as you go. Perhaps the holidays came around and you had a little extra to eat that you need to lose now on the weight loss journey. Perhaps your company is restructuring and you may not have a job, much less that promotion that you wanted. You need to take some time on a regular basis and consider if the goals are still the ones that you want to go for or if you need to make some adjustments with them. This is not an excuse to get rid of them or to give up, but it can help you to take a good hard look at what is going on and see if you really need to adjust so you don't end up failing.

- Make the goals realistic: of course, you need to make sure that the goals you are setting up are as realistic as possible, for you. It is supposed to be something of a challenge, but you should be able to realistically get to that goal if you work really hard. You have to recognize what some of your own strength and weaknesses are ahead of time and then this is much easier to figure out what you are able to do.

- Make sure they are measurable: it is not a good idea for you to pick out a goal that you are not able to measure. How are you supposed to know if you are moving forward with it or not? It is not enough to say I want to lose weight; how much weight do you want to lose and by when? It is not enough to say, I want to be rich; how rich is enough for you and how long do you want it to take. Your goals need to be something that you are able to measure so that you are able to see if you are getting close to them or not.

- Keep track: how are you supposed to know if you are reaching the goals that you want if you aren't even keeping track of the progress? Have some method down that will allow you to keep track of where you are in the goal. When you reach one of the milestones that you wrote down, make sure to see it as a big deal and celebrate a little bit. It is a lot of work to stick with a goal that you want to meet and if you are good at sticking with it and reach a major milestone that is worth celebrating and recording as well.

Goals may seem like they are not worth your time or that you could find something better to do, but in reality, they are so important. When you set goals, you are focusing your mind on doing something that is good for you; you are giving yourself some self-love in a manner that you may not have thought about in the past. It can take some time to get to the goal, but you are going to feel so much better when you have an action plan in place to help you out.

Chapter 8: Challenge Yourself

Life is hard. There are always a million things that we need to get done on a daily basis, and we may feel that we are already overworked and need to just relax and do nothing else. Relaxing is a great thing to do, it is a way to recharge and to get ourselves ready to take on a brand new day. But it is not an excuse to give up on what we want to do and not do any work at all. When we aren't challenged, we often aren't taking care of ourselves either. We may just sit there and watch the day go by, assuming that this is as good as it gets for us and that we are going to be lost and confused without any assistance.

But when we start to bring a new challenge into our days, something that makes our minds think a bit, not something that is going to harm us, we are able to see ourselves start to grow and change so much. It is too easy to just sit back and assume that things are going to change, but unless we challenge ourselves and try to see this difference, nothing is ever going to make a difference.

There are quite a few ways that you are able to challenge yourself and the method that you use is going to vary compared to the method that someone else is going to use. Here are some simple things that you can try out that will provide a good challenge to your life without making you feel overwhelmed or causing any harm to your body or mind.

Learning a brand new language

Learning a new language is a great way to challenge the mind. Learning these languages will help you to pick up a new skill, learn about a new culture, and to see the world in a whole new way. There are countless new languages that you can learn and you don't even need to become an expert in them to get the results. You can choose to go with something like Spanish, Mandarin, Hangul, German, Italian, or something else. There are countless languages and spending a few minutes each day trying to pick up one of these languages is going to help you to broaden your horizons while challenging the brain at the same time. You can choose to just stick with one language and get it mastered, or expand out to doing a new one each year or so to keep things interesting and changing.

Do something you are scared of each week

Each of us has something that we are scared of doing. We may not be the best at talking to people or we could have issues with being alone, being in dark places, or doing something else. But when we learn how to face some of those things that we are scared of, it become so much easier to live our lives and the challenge is good for our self esteem.

Let's say that you are in sales, but you aren't that fond of talking to people over the phone or in person. This could be a big problem in sales because you are definitely not going to make your money talking to people online. Instead of letting this fear get the best of you, it is time to face it for at least a few minutes a day. With the sales example, we would try to spend a good five minutes each day to call a new prospect or two and see if we could make a sale. The more times that you are able to do this, and the longer the amount of time, you will get used to it and the challenge won't seem as bad any longer. You are able to make changes to this so that it works no matter what things you are scared of.

Take up a new class or a hobby

While you are able to pick out any hobby that you would like, make sure that it is not related to your current career. You don't want to spend your free time doing the same thing that you are doing at work, plus you want to be able to expand out your horizons a bit here and that isn't going to happen if you stay in the same frame of mind. There are many great examples of classes and hobbies that you can take up including graphic design, painting, sewing, and cooking.

Now, you can do so many things with this hobby that you are trying to take up. Sometimes it is just a nice challenge that you can try and it is a great way to meet some new people. In addition, you could take this hobby and turn it into a side job, allowing you to make some extra income so that you can reach your goals (which we will talk about later on).

Try some seminars

Challenging yourself in your career is a great way to see some results in your life, and that can make you feel amazing as well. You don't have to settle for the current position you have in your job, even if you don't have the experience right now to go on with something else. You can teach yourself how to get further in your job, with or without the help of your current employer. This challenge is going to ask you to go to at least one seminar a month that is related to your career so you can make a big difference in your knowledge base and maybe even get that promotion.

When you pick out a conference, it is best right now to just stick with ones that are relevant to the industry that you work in. When you are there, you need to take time to absorb the lesson, ask questions, and connect with some of the speakers and the other people who are attending this seminar. This is going to be great for you and expanding your network can help you out, even if the information is nothing new to you.

Make some challenges with the budget

Budgeting is a hard challenge for a lot of people, but you will find that it can be a great one for helping you to reach some of your goals and it can feel good when you get enough control to cut something out of your life so that you have extra money at the end of the month. For this one, we are going to take a break from our current budget and try to develop one that is better for ourselves. One thing that many people don't understand is that money management is not always about the number on your paycheck, but it is what you are doing with the money that you get each month.

For this one, we are going to produce our current budget, either writing it out on paper or inside of the Excel system. Then you will be able to identify some of the items that you are spending money on. Learn how to cut back on this item, or cut it out completely if you are able to, and then take that money and leave it either in an emergency fund or in your new investment fun. Over time, this is going to grow and while it was a challenge to let go of some of the things that you used to enjoy, this is a great way to see some results.

Spend some time working out

You don't necessarily need to spend all of your time at the gym to get in a good workout, but ten minutes or more a day will make a big difference. Doing some dancing around the house, walking around the block, or doing something simple will help you to feel better. Aside from helping you to keep your weight in check, this exercise program is going to help release some of the happy endorphins that you need and you are going to love the way that your body looks when you are done.

Try something new

Too many times we get into a rut because we are used to doing things a certain way. We may have a routine that we like and we don't want to change it up. This routine, even though it isn't challenging us or letting us out of the negative thoughts that are everywhere, is something that feels safe to us, and most of us are going to feel really uncomfortable if we are asked to go out of this routine and do something a little bit different.

But if you would really like to challenge yourself and make a difference in your world view, and of your personal view, you need to make sure that you try out something new. This can be anything that you like. Sometimes it could be something crazy, but even something that is as simple as trying out a new restaurant, watching a type of movie that you may not have been interested in beforehand. If a crazy opportunity comes up, there is nothing wrong with giving that a try as well, but there is nothing wrong with keeping it simple and just going a little bit out of your routine and comfort zone on occasion.

Challenging yourself is a great way to ensure that you are doing things that are good for you, and will help to make your mind and your body feel better than ever before. The point of a challenge is not to bring you down and make you feel like there is something wrong with you, but they are meant to make you step a bit outside of your comfort zone so that you can really get to the good life that you deserve.

Chapter 9: Learn How to Say No

If you are like many other people, you will find that it is really hard to say no when someone asks you to help them out, take on another project, or do something else for them. When you are at work, you are already swamped and trying to get things done so that you can head out the door, and then your boss comes in and asks if you can take on another project, stay late for another meeting or just work a bit longer to help out the team.

When your child asks for another toy, asks to go and hang out with friends, asks for something else for supper even though you already spent over an hour getting it all cooked up for them, you may find that you will give in just to make things easier and not have to get into a fight.

When your spouse needs help with another project around the house or they have to stay out late so now you miss out on being with friends or having a little break, you are there to help out because you are a part of a team. When you already have a million things to do, but your kids or your friend, or your parent needs a ride so you stop by and grab them or add another errand to your list to help them out. When there is another family party that you have to go to (Yay! Your third cousin's fifth kid is having their first birthday party that they will never remember), you decide to go because someone asks. And the cycle just keeps on going and going with you always having one more thing to take care of.

While all of this stuff is keeping you busy, is it really allowing you to have much time for yourself? Sure you love all of these other people and you want to be there to help them out, but sometimes you need to take a step back and realize that you are just too busy to be there to help someone else out right at that moment. And how many of them (outside of if your child is a baby or a toddler and can't do it), are there to help you out when you ask for it?

If you really think about the answer, it may surprise you a little bit. You may realize that while you are doing all this running around and it may have become something that others expect of you by this point, none of them are necessarily ready to run around and help you out either. A few of them might, but it is more likely than not that people are expecting more out of you than you are out of them, and even if you asked, some of them may make up excuses or always be too busy to come and be there for you.

All of this is going to start draining on you over time. It is good to help others out and be there for them, but you can't give up all of yourself to do this all the time. You are important too and if your time is already swamped, why would you want to give the little bit of free time that you have to someone else?

Think of it this way, each time that you say yes to something new, you are sacrificing something. You are sacrificing time with your friends, time with your kids, time to relax at home with your spouse and take a nice hot bath. There is always a sacrifice when it comes to saying yes to others and you need to decide if this is a sacrifice that you are willing to make.

Of course, there are going to be times when you say yes to those around you. There is nothing wrong with helping out others and being here for others when they need you, but you also have to consider whether you are doing it because you feel obligated to rather than because you really have the time and the want to help them out. If you are just doing things because you feel obligated to help, you are causing a lot of pain and suffering in your own life and this could end up making it really hard to love yourself.

Chapter 10: Appreciate the Little Things in Life

Too often in our lives, we are on the run, trying to get to the big moments that are going on, rather than slowing down and enjoying some of the small things. We want to get that big promotion, have that big house, and show everyone how amazing we are, but we never stop and think about the little things that we already have and that shape who we are as a person.

When we are too busy trying to get more and more, we are really causing a lot of stress on ourselves. We may have thoughts of being inadequate and assuming that we are the reason that things aren't working out. It is really hard to have thoughts about self-love if we are constantly feeling bad because we don't' have as many materialistic things as someone else.

Learning how to appreciate the little things in life will make such a big difference in how much happiness we have. There are so many little things that are in our lives, but we mostly ignore them because we assume they are not all that important or we are too busy focusing on the big things that may never happen. But when we stop and enjoy these smaller things, we see how truly lucky and blessed we are to be alive.

So what are some of the ways that we will be able to appreciate some of the little things in our lives? Let's look at some examples:

- Keep a journal: each day, write down five to ten things that you are thankful for in your life. These don't have to be big grand gestures to be successful, they just need to be something that you are grateful for. When you take the time to think about all the good little things in your life, it is easier to get a big boost in your mood. When you immerse the mind in all of this good stuff, you are going to feel more content.

- Create a gratitude folder: this could be like a bulletin board where you are going to put up some small reminders of all the things that make you feel grateful. This could be something like a thank you note from a client, a letter from a friend, pictures of your kids, or something else. When the year is over, you can put all of the items into a brand new folder, allowing you to review the year and see just how blessed you are in life.

- Practice this gratitude with your family: a good way to do this is to establish a new gratitude practice with your family during the meal times. Each of you can go around the table and talk about how the day was, what you feel grateful for, and even share some personal stories. This shows others that you are grateful for them and makes it easier for you all to get a chance to shine.

- Turn it into a habit: you could connect your gratitude so that it becomes a daily habit. When you are brushing your teeth or getting dressed in the morning, consider listing out all of the things that you are grateful for. This makes it easier to remember that you need to do this each day.

- Keep it small: the things that you are grateful for each day do not need to be huge things. You are used to appreciating these big things and it isn't really anything new to take time out of your day to remember to appreciate them again. Start with things that are small, such as the laughter of your kids, seeing someone smile at you, the sound that rain makes when it is falling, sunshine, or even the smell of coffee or cookies baking near you. There are so many small things to appreciate and feel grateful about during the day, so learn how to concentrate on those.

- Say thank you each day: find someone you are thankful for, and make sure to let them know. It could be someone who helped you to finish a project at work; it could be to your children for helping to clean up the house, or to your spouse who helped to make dinner. You can send these out in notes, emails, or in person, but just make sure that you show your appreciation often.

- Be present: it is not enough to just be around and doing things that are a part of your routine. You also need to take the time to actually be present. You may be going through the motions of some of your daily activities, but you are probably spending that time thinking about what to make for supper, worrying about the bills, and concentrating on a whole host of other things. This makes it hard to do your job the correct way and can wear you down overall. A good solution to dealing with this is to learn how to be present. When you are doing an activity, think just about that activity and nothing else. It can take some time to get this all down, but once you learn how to be present in your daily activities, it is going to be so much easier to enjoy life and to get more out of the little things that you are blessed with.

- Take a walk in nature: if all the stress and the other work is getting to you, it may be time to take a break and try to go out in nature. Even just a walk around the block is going to help, although a nice nature walk could be even better. This is going to allow you a chance to get outside and hear the birds, feel the wind, and clear your head from all the issues that may be bothering you. There is no better way to gain appreciation for the things that are in your life than taking half an hour or more to just be in nature.

- Spend time with your family: too often we spend all of our free time at work or trying to get the house cleaned and run errands. But if we are just concentrating on those things, it is hard to get to enjoy it with the people that matter. Try to carve out at least a little bit of your day where you are able to spend it just with your family, with the phones of and not doing any chores or other work. You will never regret the time that you spend with your family, but you will regret it if you miss out on this time.

Sometimes the biggest reason that you are not able to give yourself some self-love is because you are missing out on some of the little things that are going on in your life. Self-love also includes being able to appreciate the things that you have going on in your life. If you follow some of the advice that is above, you will see that it makes a big difference in how much you enjoy the little things and even your sense of self-

love   will   get   better.

Conclusion

Self love is so important when it comes to taking care of ourselves. Too many times we spend our lives trying to be there for everyone else and help them out, but then we forget that we also need to care about ourselves as well. We are there for our friend when they feel like they failed or that they aren't good looking or something else, but then we will turn around and say even meaner things about ourselves. This is not a healthy or happy way to live our lives and it is making us miserable.

One of the best ways to add some more self love to our lives is to learn how to take care of ourselves. We must recognize that some of the behaviors that we are currently dealing with are not healthy and that we may need to make some changes to them. We need to do things that make us feel good, that allow us to be happy and thankful for all the good stuff that we have in life, rather than dwelling on the negatives in our lives or that we think are all around us about ourselves.

This also means that we need to learn how to take care of ourselves, and not just take care of everyone else around us It is fine to spend some time on something that you love. It is fine to tell people no when you want a break or you are overwhelmed. You are just as important as anyone else and learning when you can help someone and when you need to just take care of yourself can be one of the first steps to showing yourself the self love that you deserve.

Thank you and go ahead and start loving yourself today!